MW01026222

OLE & LENA JOKES

by Red Stangland

published by
NORSE PRESS

Box 1554
Sioux Falls, SD 57101
U.S.A.

Illustrated by
Marian Henjum

ISBN 0-9613274-2-1

EIGHTH PRINTING

FOREWORD

Before we commence laughing at the antics of everyone's favorite ethnics, Ole and Lena, let us pause to reflect on all the stalwart immigrants these two Scandinavians represent.

First of all, let us emphasize that "Ole & Lena Jokes" is not intended in anyway to demean or poke fun at our Norwegian, Swedish or Danish ancestors. Nor is the intent to ridicule the accents and speech patterns of folks who were born in another land and valiantly worked to learn a brand new language.

Rather, it is in loving memory of the brave new Americans who came to the U.S. and Canada to find a new life for themselves and their families that this book is written.

It was from such a family that I came, my mother and father both having been born and reared in Norway. In fact, my dad's name was Ole, and so was my grandfather on my mother's side. My great-great grandfather, Ole Peterson Norheim fathered 18 children! My own dad sired 13! So, it is easy to see how Norway got over-populated and why they had to emigrate to America back in the 1800's.

Arriving in this country, and without benefit of schooling, all the Oles and Lenas buckled down, worked hard and tried mightily to conquer the English language. It brings a tear to my eye to recall the way my mother sometimes mangled English words, speaking a sort of "Norglish." I would give anything to hear her voice again. The same for my dad.

So, in the spirit of love and respect, let us celebrate the Scandinavian sense of humor that makes a funny joke out of the many troubles and tragedies of life. For as Ole might say, "Ve might as vell enjoy life...ve vill never get out dis vorld alive anyvay."

Red Stangland
November 1986

Ole was asked to play a part in the local Fourth of July pageant. He had one line: "Hark, is that a cannon I hear?" For weeks he practiced the line constantly. It got on Lena's nerves, hearing him wander about the house trying different ways of saying, "Hark, is that a cannon I hear?" Finally, the Fourth rolled around, and Ole was standing on the stage in the city park in front of a large crowd. Suddenly, BOOM!! the cannon went off.

Ole said, "Vhat in da hell vas dat noise?"

Ole got a job in the fertilizer factory. The boss tried to determine the extent of Ole's abilities. "Tell me, do you know anything about nitrates?"
Answered Ole... "All I know is dey are cheaper dan da day rates."

A Norwegian was hitchhiking and was given a ride in a pickup truck by two Swedes. While the Norwegian was riding in the back of the pickup, the Swedes accidentally drove into the river. The Swedes got out, but the Norwegian drowned because he couldn't get the tailgate open.

Ole and Lena had many parrots over the years, each with its own particular vocabulary. One of them knew many 4 and 10 letter words and was prone to use them frequently. They kept him covered up on Sunday, as he tended to stay quiet in the dark, and they didn't want to listen to all that swearing on the Sabbath.

Once on a Tuesday the minister happened to stop by. Lena and the minister had just sat down when Lena remembered the parrot. She jumped up suddenly to get the cover, and as she started to put it over the cage, the parrot commented, "Well, that was a damned short week."

Ole came home one day and found Lena in bed with another man. Furious, Ole went to the dresser drawer and reached in for his .38 pistol. He then held the gun to his head as he confronted Lena in the bed. Lena commenced laughing hysterically. "Don't laugh, voman," said Ole. "YOU'RE NEXT!"

Doctor (on the phone): Ole, I have to tell you...your check came back.
Ole: Vell, let me tell YOU sumting. So did my artritis!

At the Ladies Aid, the discussion was on the question of "When does life begin?" Mrs. Knutson stated her opinion: "At birth." Mrs. Torkelson said she thought life began at conception. Lena, however, had an entirely different opinion. "Life begins," said Lena, "ven da dog dies and da kids leave home."

Lars asked Ole what he was going to have for supper. "Same old ting, I suppose," said Ole. "Cold shoulder and hot tongue."

Knute met Ole on the street one day. He said, "What's new, Ole?" "Vell," said Ole. "My vife yust ran off with my best friend. I'm sure going to miss him."

Our Norwegian friends down in Decorah, Iowa, have reported a break-in at the local police department. All the toilets were stolen from the police headquarters. Our Decorah source says the police have NO clues. In fact, we are told, THEY HAVE NOTHING TO GO ON.

A farm magazine reporter asked around the community whether there was a farmer in the area who was outstanding in his field. Several people mentioned Ole. So the reporter got the directions to Ole's farm. When he located the farm, sure enough. There was Ole, out standing in his field.

Ole was hunting big game in Africa when he suddenly came screaming through the jungle. "What's the matter?" asked the guide. "A lion bit off my big toe," said Ole. "Which one?" asked the guide. "How vould I know, said Ole, "Dose lions all look da same to me."

Ole, about to get married, asked his cousin what he should do on the wedding night. The cousin, a bit too reserved to be explicit, merely advised, "After you get your clothes oft, just rub her stomach and say, 'I love you, I love you.' The rest will come natural." So, after the wedding, the couple retired to their room where they disrobed. Ole remembered the instructions, so he rubbed his new bride's stomach, saying, "I love you, I love you." "Lower...Lower...," said the bride excitedly. So Ole spoke again but in a much deeper bass voice, "I LOVE YOU, I LOVE YOU."

Ole had his car towed into town when the motor quit. He told Sven about it, complaining about the outlandish price of $35. "Dat's a big robbery, Ole," said Sven. "Yah, I know it's a yip, but I got even. I kept da brakes on all da vay back to town."

Ole says that even though we are in the middle of a sexual revolution, it's just his luck to be out of ammunition.

Ole took his five little boys to church. The preacher remarked: "Such a nice family, Ole. Looks like you got a boy every single time."
"No," answered Ole. "Sometimes ve didn't even get a ting."

Lena was riding on an elevator back in the days when there were no push buttons to operate them...just an operator. Lars Pederson happened to be the operator when Lena got on. Poor Lars was trying to get the hang of starting and stopping the elevator since it was his first day on the job. With Lars at the controls, the elevator dropped through space at a dizzying speed. Lars then threw on the brake and brought the car to a shuddering halt.
"Did I stop too qvick? asked Lars.
"Oh no, indeed," said Lena. "I alvays vear my bloomers down around my ankles."

Lena mistakenly took some sugar pills for "the pill." She now has the sweetest baby in town.

Sven: How did Lena greet you vhen you came home late from da lodge smoker last night?
Ole: Oh, she got somevhat historical.
Sven: Don't you mean HYSTERICAL?
Ole: No...she got historical and brought up all my past sins.

Ole and Lena were in a bad car wreck. Since Ole died a day before Lena, he was first at the Pearly Gates. St. Peter greeted him and said, "We have to ask you one question...did you ever cheat on your wife when you were on earth?"

"Not even vunce," answered Ole.

"Good," said St. Peter. "You can have that Rolls Royce automobile over there to travel around heaven."

That was fine with Ole, so he took off to look things over. In the meantime, a Swede died and came to the Pearly Gates. St. Peter explained that he would have to tell how many times he had cheated on his wife while on earth. The Swede answered, "Only four times." So, St. Peter said, "Well, in that case, you had better take that Moped over there. The Swede took off on the litte two wheeler and eventually came across Ole with his big, luxurious Rolls Royce car. "Boy," said the Swede admiringly, "you sure got a swell car. I'll bet you were really surprised." Said Ole, "Yah, I vas surprised...but not half as surprised as vhen I saw Lena on a skate board."

Ole: Says, Lena...dis jacket you got me for
my birthday   is yust too loud.
Lena: Dat's okay, Ole...I'll get you a muffler
to gviet it down.

Lena flunked her drivers test. She opened the car door to let
out the clutch.

Ole and Lena, while in the drug store, spied a
display of Milk of Magnesia, which pro-
claimed in the poster, "Makes you feel
youthful." Ole thought he would like to feel
younger, so he bought a bottle and immediately drank it down. As they strolled
down the road toward home, Lena asked him
every few minutes whether he felt youthful as
yet. After about a mile and a half, she asked
him again: "Ole, do you feel youthful now?"
"Vell," said Ole, "I don't know dat I feel so
yout'ful...but I just did something awful
childish."

The Doctor asked Ole when he discovered he had
diarrhea.
Said Ole, "Ven I took off my bicycle clips."

Lena and Ole stood up for the wedding of Lars and Helga. Shortly after the wedding, the newlyweds moved away. Ole and Lena didn't see their friends for six years, and at the reunion at their home in Wisconsin, Lars and Helga showed off their five children. Helga was so proud, and as she confided to Lena: "Yah, Lena, it sure vas lucky I got married six years ago...becoss as it turned out, I VAS CHOCK FULL OF BABIES!"

Ole says he has developed "Oldtimers Disease." He explains that it is something like Furniture Disease ..."that's when your chest falls down into your drawers."

Ole and Lena's daughter Katrina told the folks that she planned to marry Sven because "he makes his living with his pen." Ole and Lena thought that must mean he is an author or journalist. As it turned out, he raises pigs.

Lena reports that Ole has "Dunlap's Disease." Says Lena, "His belly dun-laps over his belt."

Ole says that Lena is "yust like an angel. She's always up in the air, and harping on something."

Lena, with her hair in curlers, ran out the back door, shouting at the garbage man.
Lena: Am I too late for the garbage?
Garbage Man: No. Hop right in.

Ole's little boy, Ole Jr. is depressed. He heard someone say, "Like father, like son."

Ole has discovered a new birth control method. Lena takes off her make-up.

Ole likes the Italians because an Italian family saved his life by hiding him in their basement all during the war. It was in Mankato.

Lena wanted to lose weight. The doctor recommended she ride a horse every day. The first week, the horse lost 10 pounds.

Ole got mad at Little Ole for all his tricks. Last week, the little guy put Crazy Glue in Ole's Preparation H.

OLE HAD HIS HEART SET
ON WIRE FRAMES.

Swede: Ole, stand in front of my car and tell me if my blinkers are working.
Ole: yes...no...yes...no...yes...no... yes...no...yes...no

Lars: Do you enjoy bathing beauties, Ole?
Ole: Vell, I don't know..I've never bathed any.

Ole went to an eye doctor to have his eyes checked for glasses. The doctor directed him to read various letters with the left eye while covering the right eye. Ole was so mixed up on which eye was which that the eye doctor is disgust took a paper sack with a hole to see through, covered up the appropriate eyes and asked Ole to read the letters. As he did so, he noticed the Norwegian had tears streaming down his face. "Look," said the doctor, "there's no need to get emotional about getting glasses." "I know," agreed Ole, "But I kind of had my heart set on vire frames."

Two Norwegians brought their wives on a trip to America. They were soon trying to adopt American customs...in fact, Lars even suggested to Ole that they swap partners "like they do in America." So they did. About 11:30 that night, Lars asked to Ole..."I vonder how da vimmen folks are getting along."

Little Ole was having trouble with his arithmetic. When Great Grandpa came in the room, Little Ole said, "Grandpa, vill you help me find da common denominator?"
"Uff Da," grumbled Great Grandpa, "Dey vere looking for dat ting vhen I vas in school! Haven't dey found it yet?"

Ole went to the doctor to see if he could get help for his ulcers. The doctor reminded Ole that he has been suffering from the condition for quite some time and that unless something could be done for him, it might be fatal. "Ole," said the doctor, "I'm going to give it to you straight. Unless you get some immediate help, I'm afraid that you are not long for this world."
"Gosh," said Ole, "Vhat do you tink I can do?"
"Mothers milk is the only thing that can help you. I just happened to remember that Lena, on the other side of town, has recently had a baby. I'm sure she has enough so she can spare some for you."
So, Ole went to see Lena who assured Ole there was plenty for him. In fact, she suggested that he take the feeding direct, which Ole proceeded to do.
Before long, Lena began to breathe a little heavy and suggested, "Ole, maybe dere is something you vould like to go vid it?" Ole paused for a moment, wiped off his chin, and said, "Yah...haff you got any cookies?"

Ole: Ven I vas a little boy ve slept in a bed dat vas tvelve feet long and nine feet vide. Vot do you tink about dat?
Lars: I tink dat is a lot of bunk!

Street Evangelist: "How would you like to be a Jehovah's witness?"
Ole: "Heck, I didn't even see the accident."

Ole was experiencing fading health so he went to a doctor. "Your hearing is getting terrible," said the doctor, "and you've got to give up smoking, drinking and chasing women."
"Ridiculous!" exclaimed Ole. "Give up all that just so I can hear a little better?"

Karl: Ole, vhen did you start vearing a girdle?
Ole: Da same day my vife found vun in my glove compartment.

Little Ole went to church with his papa one Sunday. "Papa, vhat is dat board up on da vall?" asked little Ole. "Dose are da names of da members who died in da service," answered Papa. "Vhich vun," asked little Ole, "Da 8:30 or da 9:45?"

Ole, the Norwegian hired man, was called into the bedroom of the lady of the house..."Ole," she said, "take off my dress." Ole complied. "Now, Ole...take of my stockings." Ole did. "Now, Ole take off my brassiere and panties." Again Ole obeyed. "Now, Ole," said the Boss' wife, "next time you go into town, you wear your OWN clothes."

After the factory whistle blew, Ole and his work mate decided to have a beer. "Let's go to that bar across the street," suggested Ole. "You sit on a stool with a number on it; and if they call your number, you get to go upstairs and have free sex." "Wow," exclaimed the other, "Have you ever won?" "Not yet," said Ole. "But my wife has won six times already.'

Ole ran a gas station, and one day he had to clean off a windshield that had been messed up by birds. "All I can, say," he was hear to comment, "is dat it's a good ting dat cows can't fly."

Ole calls Lena his "Melancholy Baby" because she has a head like a melon and face like a Collie.

When Ole was courting Lena, they spent the day at the beach, watching the ocean roll in. In a poetic mood, Ole waxed eloquent: "Roll on, thou wild and restless ocean! Roll on!" After a brief pause, Lena looked adoringly at Ole and said, "Oh Ole! It's DOING it!"

Doctor: Your leg is swollen, but I wouldn't worry about it.
Ole: If your leg vas svollen, I vouldn't vorry about it eeder.

"WAITER, WHY IS YOUR FINGER
IN MY SOUP?"

Ole was being served in a fancy restaurant. "Vaiter," said Ole, "Why is your finger in my soup?" "I injured my finger today," answered the waiter, "and my doctor said to keep it in a warm place." "Vell," snorted Ole, "vhy don't you put it vhere da sun don't shine?" "I do," answered the waiter, "when I'm out in the kitchen."

Lars: Say Ole. I went by your house last night and noticed you kissing your wife in the window.
Ole: The yoke's on you. I vasn't even home last night.

Lena: Vhen ve vere younger, Ole, you used to nibble on my ear.
(Ole starts to leave the room)
Lena: Vhere are you going, Ole?
Ole: Into da bedroom to get my teeth.

Ole says: "Never tell people your troubles. Half of dem don't care...and da odder half is glad it happened to you."

Ole: Vaitress...bring me some vatery scrambled eggs, den burn some toast, den bring me some veak coffee.
Waitress: Yes sir, right away.
Ole: Don't be too fast...and vhile you're at it...nag me awhile..I'm homesick for my vife.

LARS SAW OLE
KISSING HIS WIFE
IN THE WINDOW.

19

Two Norwegians were trying to train their Bird Dog. Said Nels: "Trow him up yust unce more, Ole, an' if he don't fly dis time, yust shoot him."

Ole stopped in at a bait shop and inquired as to the cost of worms.
"One dollar for all you need," said the propietor.
"O.K." answered Ole. "Give me two dollars worth."

Lena got a phone call from her husband Ole, announcing he has purchased a condominium.
"Good," she told a neighbor lady. "Now I can throw away my diagram."

Lena: You don't love my anymore! All you ever think about is golf. I bet you don't even remember the day we were married.
Ole: Of course I do. Dat vas da day I sank dat 40-foot putt.

Lars: I hear you bought a farm for yourself, Ole.
Ole: Yah, I got fifty five cows and one bull.
Lars: Is that so? You're a pretty independent man now, aren't you?
Ole: Not half as independent as that bull.

Lena doesn't worry about Ole chasing women. She says, "Da dog chases cars, but he don't know how to drive."

Ole and Lena took a monkey in to live with them. A neighbor stopped in and took a look at their new pet. "Yah, he even eats at the table vid us," said Ole. "And at night, he sleeps in da bed between me and Lena." The neighbor looked somewhat astonished and inquired, "But what about the smell?" "Vell," said Ole, "he'll have to get used to it yust like I did."

Ole is so cheap that after landing safely in an airplane, he grumbled, "Well, there goes $5 down the drain for flight insurance."

Ole: I better go home...my wife is in bed with Laryngitis.
Sven: Is dat Greek back in town again?

The fire department got a fire call, and it was from Ole. "How do we get out to your place, Ole?", inquired the fire chief.
"Vell," said Ole, "You might use dat little red truck you got dere at da fire station."

Ole and Lena, who had recently been married, were driving along the road when Lena began feeling amorous.

"Ole, let's stop da car and have ourselves a good time," suggested Lena.

"How in da vorld could ve do dat?" exclaimed Ole. Ve're out in public. Everybody vould see us."

"Vell, dat's no problem," answered Lena. "ve can yust get under da car."

"Yah, but vhat if somebody comes by and says sumting?" Ole commented.

"Vell, in case somebody stops and asks vhat you are doing, yust say you're fixing da clutch."

So, Lena finally convinced Ole, and they stopped the car and got under it. As they were commencing to have a good time, Lars Olson walked by and said, "Ole, vhat in da vorld are you doing?"

"Can't you see I'm under here fixing da clutch?" said Ole.

"Vell," responded Lars. "You better vork on da brakes first...da car has rolled half a block down da street."

Ole was trying to land his boat but the choppy water was making it difficult. Just as it appeared that Ole might land in the water, Lars, up on shore yelled: "Yump, Ole! Yump."

Responded Ole: "How can I yump ven dere's no place to stood?"

Lena was being examined by the doctor.
"Ever been in the hospital?" inquired the doc.
"No...never in my life," answered Lena.
"Ever been bed ridden?" inquired the doctor.
"Yah," answered Lena with a smile, "Dozens
of times...and tvice in a buggy."

Ole was given a bottle of medicine for his hearing problem. It must have worked, because two days later he
heard from his uncle in Norway.

Lena went into a drug store and asked for
talcum powder.
"Yes maam...walk this way," said the druggist, walking briskly down the aisle.
"Uff Da," said Lena, "If I could valk dat vay, I
vouldn't need da talcum powder."

Lars and Ole were childhood friends. They didn't see
each other for nearly 50 years. "Yah, Ole," said Lars, "I
can remember our childhood like it was yesterday.
Remember ven ve vould valk to Sunday School togedder? Ve vould have da teacher read us stories, den ve
vould color in a book. And den ve vould say da Lord's
prayer. Ole, can you still say da Lord's Prayer?" "Yah
shure," said Ole, "Now I lay me down to sleep..."

Ole went into the fertilizer business and
became rather successful. "In fact," he told
Blomquist, "I guess you could say ve are
number vun in number two."

OLE WANTS TO BE BURIED AT SEA.

Doctor: You seem to be healthy for a man of 75. How is your love life?
Ole: Vell, almost every day.
Doctor: That's remarkable. Tell me more.
Ole: Vell, almost on Monday, almost on Tuesday, almost on Wednesday, and so on.

You've heard about bad cooks...Lena actually keeps Alka Seltzer on tap.

Lena mistakenly took some sugar pills for "the pill." She now has the sweetest baby in town.

Sven: Have you heard...dat dey elected a Pole to be Pope?
Ole: Yah, it's about time...dose Catlicks have had it long enough.

Undertaker: What can we do for you?
Ole: I vant to make arrangements for my funeral to be buried at sea.
Undertaker: Why do you want to be buried at sea?
Ole: To get back at my vife. She said dat vhen I die, "she is going to dance on my grave!"

Ole appeared with five other men in a rape case police line-up. As the victim entered the room, Ole blurted, "Yep... that's her!"

Ole says: "I never knew vhat happiness vas until I got married. By dat time, it vas too late."

Ole and Lena took a Caribbean cruise one winter. One day as they sauntered around the ship, they poked their heads into a lounge where the passengers were being entertained by a ventriloquist act. Much to Ole's annoyance, they were telling Norwegian jokes.

Ole strutted up toward the stage. "Yust a golldarn minute dere! You got a lotta nerve tellin' yokes on da Norvegians! I know all kinds of dem, and dey're all hard-vorking, upstanding people! You got no call trying to make dem out to be stupid!"

The ventriloquist was apologetic. "I'm sorry you feel that way, sir. Certainly I didn't intend any disrespect. I was just..."

Ole cut him short. "I vasn't talking to you. I vas talking to dat little hahn-yocker sittin' on your lap."

Lena: Ole, let's go jogging togedder.
Ole: How come?
Lena: Vell, because my doctor told me I could lose veight by vorking out with a dumb-bell.

Little Sven was sucking his thumb. Lena told him, "If you keep doing dat, you'll svell up like a balloon and explode." A few days later, she and Little Sven stopped in to see Tina Herringstad, who was eight months pregnant.

Little Sven looked her up and down and exclaimed, "I know vhat YOU'VE been doing."

Lena was in the bathtub when the door bell rang. "Who iss it?" she called out. "Blind man," came the answer from the front door. Lena got out of the tub, walked straight to the front door without so much as a stitch of clothes, and threw open the door. There stood a man who asked, "Where do you want me to put these blinds, lady?"

Ole and Lena lived on a farm. Ole had a new outhouse built because the old one was so decrepit. Rather than take the time to tear down the old one, he had the hired man put a stick of dynamite inside the structure. As they prepared to detonate the charge from 100 yards away by remote control, Lena came out of the house heading for the "little house." (The men had forgotten to tell her of their plans). Consequently, when Lena sat down, almost immediately the dynamite charge went off, blowing Lena (and everything else) sky high. As Lena brushed herself off, she was heard to remark, "Vell, it sure vas a good ting I didn't do dat INSIDE da house."

Brita: I heard dat Ole proposed to you and dat you accepted. Did he tell you dat he had proposed to ME first?
Lena: Vell, no; but he did mention dat he had done a lot of foolish tings before ve met.

Ole and Lena attended a Gay Nineties party. Half of the people were gay...and rest were past 90.

Lena says: "Vimmen spend one-third of their life looking for a husband...den they spend another two-thirds vundering vhere he is."

Lena was a servant girl for the Johnson family. One night she was preparing to serve dinner...and bumped into Mr. Johnson in the doorway to the dining room. Going back to the kitchen, she ran into Sonny Johnson. Both Sonny Johnson and Mr. Johnson chided her a bit for being in the way. Sensitive Lena took it to heart and went to Mrs. Johnson. Sobbing, she said, "Mrs. Yohnson...I'm going to leave here...I'm in da family's way." Misunderstanding, Mrs. Johnson exclaimed, "Why Lena...when did it happen...?" "Oh," said Lena..."it was vunce in da dining room vid Mr. Yohnson and vunce in the kitchen vid Sonny."

Ole and Lena had nine very handsome children. Then came a tenth child...but this one...to be blunt...was extremely ugly. Ole thought about it for some time, then one day, he confronted Lena. "Lena...tell me da truth...is dat last youngster really mine?" "Yah, Ole," confessed Lena. "Dat last baby is yours. But da others AREN'T."

Lena, a new bride, brought a dish for approval
of her new husband. Said she, "Da two tings I
prepare best are meatballs and peach pie..."
Ole: Hmmmm. And vhich vun is dis?

Ole: Tell me, Doctor. How do I stand?
Doctor: That's what puzzles me, Ole.

Lena: Ole, if I die first, vill you promise to ride
to da cemetery vid my mudder?
Ole: Vell, I s'pose I can. But, I'll tell you...it
vill ruin my whole day!

Ole: Everytime I flush the toilet, it nips me.
Swede: No wonder...you're sitting on a mop bucket.

Hans called Ole long distance and asked him
to loan him $5. "I can't hear you, Hans," said
Ole. "Dis line must be bad." The operator
broke in to say, "I can hear him perfectly
clear." "Vell," said Ole, "If you can hear him
so good, vhy don't YOU lend him da five
dollars."

Lena went into a drug store and asked for talcum
powder. Asked the druggist, "Mennen?" "No, silly," said
Lena... "Vimmens."

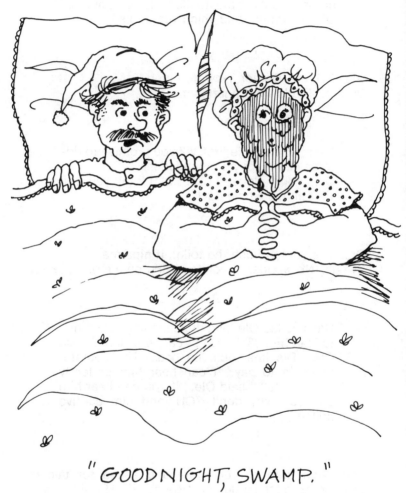

"GOODNIGHT, SWAMP."

Ole got a tattoo on his stomach reading "Mom." When his friends asked why it was done on his stomach rather than on his chest, Ole explained: "Vell, dere is more room on my stomach; and besides, I got da 'O' free."

Ole was telling about Lena's mud-pack beauty treatments. "Yah," said Ole, "at bedtime, I turn out da light and I say, 'goodnight, Swamp.'"

Ole tried to learn to be a carpenter, but he had the misfortune of burning down the house he was building when he tried to weld two 2x4's together.

Ole applied for a job at the Chicago police department. He was given test after test, but could pass none of them. Desiring to have a Norwegian in the department, as a member of a minority, the Police Captain decided to try one more test...this one with only one question, "Who shot Lincoln?" Ole answered, "I don't know." "Look," said the Captain, "take this question home and study it. Maybe when you come back tomorrow you'll know the answer." That night, the Ole's friends asked him if he got the job. "I tink I might have," said Ole. "Dey got me vorking on a murder case already."

Ole was sent to prison for one year because he was caught taking some hogs that belonged to a neighbor. The day he left the farm to go to prison was a sad one. As he bravely bid goodbye to Lena, he said, "Lena, I'm leaving you and da hired man in charge of da farm til I get back."

Upon his release, Ole happily came back to the farm where he found things in good condition and the farm thriving. Even Lena seemed in fairly good spirits as she greeted him after his 12 months away. Lena served Ole some of his favorite lutefisk and lefse. As Ole gazed around the kitchen, he spotted a jar in the cupboard with 9 dollars and five soybeans in it.

"Lena," he queried, "Vhat is dat yar vid five soybeans in it?" "Oh, Ole," said Lena, "I have a confession to make. Vhen you vas in prison, I got awfully lonesome vidout you. So vhen I couldn't stand it so good, da hired man and me, vell, ve kinda got togetdder a few times. And vhen ve did, ve put a soybean in da yar."

Ole thought a minute, and told himself that in a year's time, five occasions weren't so bad that he couldn't forgive Lena. "But Lena," said Ole, "Vhat is da nine dollars for?"

"Vell, you see, vun day da market on soybeans vas up to nine dollars, so I yust sold off a bushel."

> Lena: What ever happened to our sex relations?
> Ole: As I recall, ve didn't even get a Christmas card from dem.

Lena is so fat that when she decided to take up jogging, they made her take the truck route.

Ole decided to divorce Lena. His friend, Lars, expressed surprise. "Why are you divorcing Lena after all she's been through with you," asked Lars. "Why you went through the drouth when the grasshoppers got all of the crops that didn't burn up. Then you got a job in town and when you lost it, Lena went to work. And when you got another job and broke your hip in an accident, Lena was right there with you. And when you got in that legal trouble, why Lena stuck right with you. After all that, WHY, Ole would you divorce Lena?" Ole thought a moment, and then remarked, "Vell, I got to figuring she must be a jinx."

Ole: How much are your eggs?
Grocer: 90 cents a dozen, whole, and 40 cents for cracked.
Ole: Vell, how about cracking me a dozen?

Ole went from Duluth to Minneapolis one weekend. He met Lena and they had a good time together. A few weeks later, Ole got a call from Lena. Ole said. "How's tings vid you down in Minneapolis, Lena?" "Dat's vat I'm calling you about, Ole," said Lena. "I haven't been sick for two months." "Vell," exclaimed Ole, "Den you're lucky. Ve all haff had da flu up here in Duloot."

Why did Ole wear two jackets while painting?
Because the directions on the paint can said, "Put on two coats."

The highway patrolman stopped Ole's car and informed the Norwegian that his wife had fallen out of the car three miles back. "Thank goodness," exclaimed Ole. "I thought I'd gone deaf."

Ole says that Lena is a fast talker...300 words per minute...with gusts to 500.

Marriage license clerk: "Names, please."
Ole: Ole Johnson
Lena: Lena Johnson
Clerk: Any relations?
Lena (blushing): "Yah, vunce or tvice. Ole couldn't vait."

Little Ole, the grocery boy was filling a lady's grocery sack. "I'll yust put da eggs on da bottom of da sack, lady," he said. "Dat vay, if da eggs break, dey von't mess up da canned goods.

Ole decided to get a vasectomy because he didn't want any more grandchildren.

Ole got into a bad fight and killed a man. Lena came to see him in prison and asked what sentence had been passed. Said Ole: "Dey sentenced me to be electrocuted." Answered Lena: "Don't vorry, Ole. I'll vait for you.

Ole says, "I married my vife because of a mental problem. I vas out of my mind at da time."

Little Ole was kidnapped by a Polack... who then sent Little Ole back with a ransom note. Ole and Lena sent him back with the money.

Ole was musing on the park bench. "Vunce I had everything...a nice apartment...the love of a tender young voman. And den my vife had to valk in and spoil it."

Ole was an incurable optimist. No matter what horrible event people would tell him about, Ole would invariably say, "Vell, it could have been worse." One day two of his cronies told Ole about the terrible tragedy where Bjarne Olsson was killed by Olaf Hegermoe after Bjarne had been fooling around with Hegermoe's wife. "Vell," said Ole in his usual manner, "It could have been vorse." "Vorse? How could it have been vorse?" asked the crony. "Vell," said Ole, "If it had been da night before, it vould have been ME."

Ole was commenting on the way the world is today, "It's REELY sumting...da vay da young things go around with fancy hair-dos and skin tight pants. And da vimmen are even vorse."

Personnel Director: Before I consider you for a job, do you lie, cheat, steal or come in late?
Ole: No...I never have. But I'm villing to learn.

Here's a Norwegian Wedding announcement:
C2DV
L Mr.
(Translation: "Come to da vedding; Lena mister period")

Ole's wife had triplets...so he went out looking for the other two guys.

As Ole lay dying, he asked his wife: "Lena, vould you get me some of dat lutefisk you got cooking on da stove?" "I'm sorry," said Lena, "I'm saving dat for after da funeral."

Ole took his wife to the doctor who gave her a physical. He took Ole aside and said, "There's really nothing seriously wrong with your wife. I'd say everything would be OK is she had sex 7 or 8 times a month." "Vell," said Ole, "dat sounds fine. You could put me down for a couple times."

Lena discovered that her husband, Ole, was fooling around. She called the undertaker, saying, "I vant you to come and pick up my husband's body." Inquired the undertaker, "When did he die?" She answered, "He starts tomorrow."

Lena: Do you have any trouble making up your mind?
Tena: Yes and no.

Ole bought Lena a wig because he heard she was "getting bald" at the office.

Ole came home to his apartment one night, snorting. "Dat Yanitor, vot a bragger. He claims he's made love to every woman in dis apartment except one."
"Hmmph," said Ole's wife. "Must be that snooty Mrs. Peterson on third floor."

Ole and Lena went to a lawyer to see about getting a divorce. "How old are you folks?" asked the lawyer. "Vell, I'm 90 and Lena is 89," said Ole. "How come you are getting a divorce NOW?" asked the lawyer. Said Ole, "Ve vaited until all da kids were dead."

Ole was out of town on a trip and was delayed in getting home. When he got back the next day, Lena informed him that a burglar had broken into the house the night before by way of the bedroom.

Ole: Did he get anything?

Lena: He sure did. At first, I thought it was you.

Lena: I yust bought myself a new hat. I like to buy a hat for myself ven I'm down in the dumps.

Ole: Hmmm...I vundered vere you found it.

Ole answered the phone and soon hung up the receiver. "Who vas it," inquired Lena. "Somevun must have thought dis vas the Coast Guard. All dey said vas, "Is da coast clear?""

Bertha: Is Lena a good housekeeper?

Tina: I should say she is...she's been married three times and kept the house every time.

Ole received cuff links and a short sleeved shirt for his birthday. So he had his wrists pierced.

Ole met his friend Alfred one day in downtown Fargo. Ole told about all the problems he'd been having. His wife had run off with the preacher. His son was on drugs. His daughter was leading a life of sin. And he's had several lawsuits filed on him. Alfred responded sympathetically. "Sorry to hear about dat, Ole. By da vay, vat are you doing dese days?" "Same ting," said Ole, "selling good luck charms."

Ole was tired after driving his truck from Minneapolis to Duluth, so he stopped at a diner in Cloquet for a snack. There were five mean-looking motorcyclists from Hibbing there and they started pushing him around and poking fun at him. When the waitress brought Ole's food, these guys grabbed it from her and ate it. Ole didn't say a word. Pulled a dollar from his pocket, paid his bill and walked out. One of the cyclists said to the waitress: "That Norwegian isn't much of a man, is he." Waitress: "No, and he's not much of a truck driver either. He just ran over five motor bikes that were parked outside."

Ole was trying to make time with his girl in a Volkswagen back in his younger days. She ran outside and said, "Hurry, and get out of the car before I get out of the mood."

Ole: "I gotta get out of da mood before I can get out of da car."

OLE HAD TROUBLE WRITING
"HAPPY BIRTHDAY" ON A CAKE.

Ole and Lars were business partners and good friends. One day Lars started off for work and discovered he'd forgotten his tools. Returning home, he looked around for his wife, Lena, and finally found her in the bedroom. To his surprise, she was on the bed with no clothes on. "Vat in the vorld are you doing vidout any clothes, voman?" Lars asked. "Vel, I yust don't have any clothes to vear, dat's vhy," answered Lena. "Vat you talking about," said Lars as he opened the closet door and began counting: "Vun dress, two dress, tree dress, four dress...hello Ole...Five dress...

Ole showed up at work with a black eye. He explained it as being caused by "Seenus trouble."
"No, no," said one of his co-workers, "It's called SINUS trouble."
"Vell, all I know," said Ole, "Is that I was out with this married voman and her husband seen us."

Ole had trouble putting "Happy Birthday" on a cake. His main problem was getting the cake in the typewriter.

The nurse told Ole to strip to the waist. So he took off his pants.

Marriage Counselor: You say you are having marital problems. Do you have mutual climax? Ole: No...our insurance is Lut'ran Brudderhood.

Ole calls his wife "Crisco" because she's fat in the can.

Ole was apprehended stark naked one night on the main street of town. When collared by a policeman, Ole attempted to explain his nudity. "Vell, ve vas at a Svingers party, me and Lena. Den, some-vun said, "let's get our clothes off and go to town." So, I did, it turned out I vas da only vun dat made it into town."

Ole: I yust had my life insured for $25,000.
Lena: Dere you go again...alvays tinking of yourself.

Ole was riding the bus when a young lady addressed him. She said, "Would you mind giving your seat to a pregnant woman?"
Always the gentleman, Ole relinquished his bus seat. As he looked at the lady and reflected on the situation, Ole asked, "Yust how long have you been pregnant?"
The gal answered, "About 15 minutes, and am I TIRED!"

Ole: I know how you can sell more beer in this bar.
Bartender: You do? How?
Ole: Try filling up the glasses.

Lena: Uff Da, I don't know which I dread the most...having a tooth pulled or having a baby.
Dentist: Well, I wish you'd make up your mind so I will know which way to tilt the chair.

How do you tell the gay Norwegian from the straight Norwegian?
—The straight Norwegian likes butter, but the gay Norwegian prefers Ole.

Ole and Lena were traveling down the street in their car. A patrolman stopped them and motioned Ole to roll down the window on the driver's side.
"Sir, you were going 50 miles an hour in a 30 mile zone."
Ole: No, officer, I vas going yust 30 miles an hour.
Patrolman: Well, I say you were going 50 miles an hour.
Ole: No, I vas going yust 30 miles an hour.
Patrolman: And I say you were going 50!
Lena: (trying to be helpful) Officer, you really shouldn't try to argue with Ole when he's been drinking.

Ole reports that Lena spent two hours in the beauty salon last Tuesday. "And," says Ole, "dat vas yust for da estimate."

Ole applied for a job as a watchman at the railroad yard where two rail lines intersected. The foreman doing the hiring asked Ole some questions to determine whether he was alert enough. "Ole, what would you do if you were on the job and two trains were coming toward the junction at the same time?"

Said Ole, "I vould immediately call my brudder."

Forman: Call your brother? What in the world for?

Ole: 'Cause my brudder ain't never seen no train wreck before.

There was a Norwegian who was so dumb he ran downtown to get training wheels for his wife's menstrual cycle.

Ole: I don't stay the Holiday Inn anymore.
Sven: Why not?
Ole: Towels are too thick.
Sven: What's wrong with that?
Ole: Can't get my suitcase closed.

Know how a Norwegian lost 5 pounds? He took a bath.

Some Norwegians were playing a bunch of Swedes in a game of football. When the six o'clock whistle blew, the Swedes went home. Four plays later, the Norwegians scored a touchdown.

Lena was called for jury duty and somehow was elected foreman of the jury. When they returned from their deliberations, the judge asked, "Have you reached a verdict?"

"Yah," said Lena, "Ve find da guy dat stole da horse Not Guilty."

Lars: How's your brudder doing at dat salesman yob?
Ole: Vell, he got two orders yesterday. Get out. . . and Stay out.

How do you get a one-armed Swede out of a tree?
---You wave at him.

Ole showed up for work with bandaged ears. "What happened?" asked a fellow worker.

"Vell," said Ole, "Last night I vas ironing my shirt vhen da phone rang and I picked up da iron by mistake."

"What happened to the other ear," asked the companion.

"Oh...dat," Ole explained. "Vell, I had to call da doctor."

Ole and Lars were hunting ducks. At the end of the day, they'd had no luck. Ole turned to Lars and asked, "Do you tink ve maybe haven't been trowing da dog high enough?"

Ole and Lena had a pet parrot that could only speak one phrase: "Who is it?". Though they tried and tried, it refused to say anything but "Who is it?".

One morning Lena had a problem with a plugged drain, so she called a plumber who said he could be there at two o'clock that afternoon. By 4:00 P.M. the plumber still hadn't arrived, so Lena left to run some errands, figuring that the plumber wouldn't make it that day. The plumber showed up at 4:30 and knocked on the door. Hearing the knocking, the parrot said, "Who is it?"

"It's the plumber", the man stated. No one came to the door.

He knocked again and heard the same question from inside, "Who is it?"

This time a little more loudly, he announced, "It's The Plumber!" This drew no response. This went on 7 or 8 times, and each time the man responded more loudly and emphatically, "IT'S THE PLUMBER!!!"

The plumber decided he would give it one more try, and if no one opened the door, he would leave. He knocked again. Once again came the same inquiring voice, "Who is it?"

This time he summoned up every ounce of energy and boomed out, "IT'S THE PLUMMMMERRRR!!!!!!" and dropped dead of a heart attack on the doorstep.

Lena was still gone when Ole arrived home from work. Ole walked to the front door, noticed the dead man lying there, and said, "Yee Vhiz! I vonder who dis could be."

From inside, Ole heard a squawky voice yelling, "IT'S THE PLUMMMMERRRR!!"

Ole stopped into a local tavern and sat down with Lars and Sven, who were discussing aphrodisiacs. After listening awhile, Ole chimed in, "I don't know if I believe in dat stuff, but I do know dere is a food dat permanently lowers a voman's sex drive... It's called Vedding Cake."

There's even MORE fun waiting when you order from the book list below.

	Price	Qty.	Total
* Polish Jokes	$3.00		
* Norwegian Jokes	$3.00		
* Uff Da Jokes	$3.00		
* Ole & Lena Jokes 1	$3.00		
* More Ole & Lena Jokes 2	$3.00		
* Ole & Lena Jokes III	$3.00		
* Ole & Lena Jokes 4	$3.00		
* Ole & Lena Jokes 5	$3.00		
* Ole & Lena Jokes 6	$3.00		
* Ole & Lena Jokes 7	$3.00		
* Office Jokes (R Rated)	$2.75		
* Blonde Jokes	$2.50		
* Norwegian Book of Knowledge (Above title has blank text and humorous material on back cover)	$1.75		
* How to Become Your Own Boss ... Shortcuts on becoming self-employed	$4.95		
	GRAND TOTAL		

ALL PRICES INCLUDE POSTAGE AND HANDLING
10% DISCOUNT ON ORDERS OVER $15.00

Name _____

Address _____

_____

Send check or money order to:
NORSE PRESS, Box 1554, Sioux Falls, SD 57101